THE BIG BOOK OF
DESSERTS AND PASTRIES

Dozens of Recipes for Gourmet Sweets and Sauces

CLAES KARLSSON
PHOTOS: PEPE NILSSON
TRANSLATION: ELLEN HEDSTROM

SKYHORSE PUBLISHING

THANKS

I would like to thank Christina and Pepe for their amazing teamwork. Mariana at the Sorunda Food Hall and Stefan at Werners GourmetService for the excellent quality of their raw ingredients, you are the best! Mum and Dad, who are always so positive. NK Glass, Porcelain & Kitchen for the loan of the beautiful glassware. And last but not least, James for all the inspiration.

Claes

10 9 8 7 6 5 4 3 2 1

Library of Congress Cataloging-in-Publication Data is available on file.
ISBN: 978-1-62087-050-1

Printed in India
Photos © Pepe Nilsson
Design: Hammarqvist Design
Typeface set in Neutra – thanks www.fontbolaget.se
Reprographics: Italgraf Media

CONTENTS

CLAES
KARLSSON

FIND YOUR OWN FAVORITE!

This is the book for anyone who loves cookies, pastries, candy, or desserts. Why not try a fancy, but easy, panna cotta, the latest trend in baking (whoopie pies and cupcakes), a classic tuile or super-sticky brownie, or maybe cinnamon waffles for Sunday brunch?

By using different accompaniments, you can add further variety to the goodies. Mango sauce, toffee sauce, or a white chocolate sauce together with fresh berries can add some zing as well as a decorative look, and neither a chocolate net nor spun sugar is as hard to make as it might look.

Desserts and pastries should not be complicated. The recipes in this book are easy to follow using the equipment you already have in the kitchen and ingredients available in your regular grocery store.

Invite your family and friends or indulge yourself. Everything is possible once you have awoken the baker in you.

Good luck in the kitchen!

Claes Karlsson

A FEW TIPS BEFORE YOU START

ICE CREAM BY HAND OR MACHINE

There are several recipes for ice cream and sorbet in this book. Nothing compares to home-made ice cream made from scratch, as opposed to the often artificial taste of store-bought ice cream. The recipes recommend using an ice cream maker, as the consistency will be soft and smooth. There are several types of ice cream makers, from simple electric ones to makers with a built-in freezer. You can also make ice cream by hand, but it will take longer and the results will not be as good as when made with a machine. When the ice cream mixture is almost frozen, whip it smooth and then place it back in the freezer. Repeat a few times. When the ice cream is done, it should be kept in freezer-safe containers to prevent ice crystals from forming. Homemade ice cream should be eaten within two weeks. Another tip is to place the ice cream in the fridge an hour before serving to enhance the flavors.

FREEZING PASTRIES AND DESSERTS

All cookies, pastries, candy, and desserts taste best immediately after they have been made, although many of the dishes in this book can be frozen. Among the pastries, the white chocolate cake with blueberries as well as the cherry cake can be frozen. Brownies without toppings can also be frozen—the milk chocolate brownie, for example. A tip is to freeze cookies before baking. They can then be defrosted and baked according to the amount you need at that time. Freezing peanut brittle, vanilla toffee tart, licorice toffee, and almond biscotti is not recommended.

MELTING CHOCOLATE IN DIFFERENT WAYS

If you wish to melt chocolate using a microwave oven, break the chocolate into small bits and heat on high for a maximum of half a minute. Stir and continue in the same way until the chocolate has completely melted. It can burn quickly in the microwave if you don't keep an eye on it. You can also heat the chocolate over a pot of water. Let the water simmer and place a larger pan or bowl over the pot of simmering water. (It should not be placed in the water!) Then add the chopped chocolate to the larger pan or bowl and melt. Stir occasionally. ·

THE OVEN: CONVECTION OR NOT

If you use a convection oven, think about lowering the temperature. If it says 350 °F (180 °C) in the recipe, you can lower it by 50 °F (10 °C).

THERMOMETER

A thermometer is a good investment and a necessity for some recipes. For other recipes (for example, the licorice toffee) you can test if the toffee is ready by dropping a small amount into a glass of cold water. If it forms a solid ball, the toffee is ready.

WHISKS

An electric mixer is suitable for beating together a fluffy batter such as sugar and butter. However, a hand held mixer or a food processor with a blade works better for making a more compact batter that needs to bind—for example, a chocolate truffle.

DECORATIONS

In specialty food shops you can find fun and interesting decorative pieces that will be sure to impress your guests. Even regular grocery stores often carry a selection of decorative balls and sprinkles. And of course, you can always make your own decorations. In this book you will find recipes for fancy chocolate nets and spun sugar, as well as tricks for easy sprinkles that you can make yourself.

DESSERTS

STRACCIATELLA MERINGUE CAKE

MAKES ABOUT 14 PORTIONS

9 oz (250 g) finely chopped white chocolate
1 cup (200 ml) whipping cream
1 tbsp honey
5 cups (300 g) whipped cream
7 oz (200 g) grated dark chocolate
2 ready-made meringue bases, approx. 8 inches (20 cm) in diameter

Chocolate garnish, see page 144

Place the white chocolate in a bowl. Heat the cream on low heat, pour over the white chocolate, and leave for 5 minutes. Then, mix in the honey to form a smooth truffle. Allow to cool overnight. Stir the whipped cream lightly and mix with the grated dark chocolate. Don't stir too vigorously. Spread half of the white chocolate truffle onto the first meringue base and then spread half the whipped cream mixture on top of that. Place the second meringue base on top and repeat. Garnish with a chocolate net.

RHUBARB SOUP WITH CARDAMOM TUILES

SOUP:

2 cups (250 g) fresh or frozen rhubarb, cut into roughly
    half-inch (1 cm) pieces

1 ¾ cups (400 ml) water

1 scraped vanilla pod

TUILES:

½ cup (50 g) ground almonds

1 tbsp butter at room temperature

2 tbsp sugar

1 tbsp white syrup or glucose

1 pinch of ground cardamom

Heat the ingredients for the soup and let them simmer for approximately 20 minutes. Blend with a hand-held mixer and allow to cool. Combine the tuile ingredients and stir into a smooth batter. Place teaspoon-sized amounts of the batter onto a baking tray covered with parchment paper. Bake in the center of the oven at 350 °F (175 °C) for about 5 minutes. Make sure the soup is well chilled and serve with the tuiles.

VANILLA PANNA COTTA WITH RASPBERRY COULIS

MAKES 4 PORTIONS

1 ¾ cups (400 g) cream
1 tsp vanilla sugar
1 tbsp granulated sugar
1 gelatin leaf, soaked in cold water
1 cup (200 g) frozen raspberries
1 tbsp granulated sugar

Bring the cream and the two types of sugar to a simmer, then remove the pan from the heat. Remove excess water from the gelatin leaf and stir into the mixture. Place in serving glasses and let set in the refrigerator for at least 4 hours. Mix the defrosted raspberries with the sugar and place atop the set panna cotta as garnish.

MANGO SORBET

3 tbsp sugar
½ cup (100 ml) water
2 cups (300 g) mango (approx. 2 ripe mangos)
Fresh fruit to garnish, optional

Boil the sugar and water, then allow to cool. Combine the mango and the sugary syrup in a food processor. Mix for about 3 minutes. Freeze in an ice cream maker for around 30 minutes until smooth and firm. Serve with fresh fruit.

WHITE CHOCOLATE SORBET

MAKES 8–10 PORTIONS

2 gelatin sheets
2 cups (500 g) water
¾ cup (150 g) granulated sugar
½ cup (100 ml) honey
5.3 oz (150 g) finely chopped white chocolate
½ cup (150 ml) milk
Berries and lemon balm (a lemony herb in the mint family)
    to garnish, optional

Soak the gelatin sheets in plenty of cold water. Boil the water, sugar, and honey. Remove the pan from the heat and add the finely chopped chocolate. Let it sit for 5 minutes. Add the gelatin and stir. Allow to cool. Once cooled, add the milk to the sorbet mixture and pour into an ice cream maker. Let freeze for 40 minutes. Decorate with fresh berries and lemon balm (optional).

LEMON GRANITA

¼ cup (50 g) sugar
½ cup (100 g) water
Juice of 4 ripe lemons
6 serving glasses, pre-chilled in the freezer

Bring the sugar and water to a boil, then allow to cool. Add the lemon juice and mix thoroughly. Pour the mixture into a clean pan or bowl and freeze for 4 hours. Scrape off layers of the frozen granita using a fork to create a granular texture. Divide into pre-chilled glasses and serve immediately.

HONEY PANNA COTTA

2 cups (500 ml) whipping cream
3 tbsp honey
1 tsp muscovado sugar
3 gelatin sheets, soaked in cold water

Chocolate curls for garnish

Bring the cream to a simmer together with the honey and
sugar. Remove the pan from the heat, add the gelatin,
and stir thoroughly until dissolved. Sift the mixture
through a fine sieve and pour into serving dishes or
glasses. Cool in the fridge for at least 3 hours before
serving. Garnish with thin chocolate curls (see page 152).

VANILLA TOFFEE TART

MAKES AROUND 10

BATTER:
¾ cup (200 g) salted butter at room temperature
3 ¼ cups (400 g) flour, approx.
½ cup (100 g) confectioners' sugar
¼ cup (50 g) sugar
1 egg yolk

FILLING:
¼ cup (50 g) butter
½ cup (100 ml) cream
1 scraped vanilla pod
2 tbsp glucose or honey
¾ cup (150 g) sugar

Fresh raspberries to garnish, optional

Combine all the ingredients and stir into a smooth batter. Cover in plastic wrap and let cool in the fridge for at least 1 hour. Roll out the dough to a quarter-inch (3 mm) thickness on a well-floured surface. Line the dishes for the tarts with the dough, bake in the center of the oven at 350 °F (175 °C) for about 10 minutes, and allow to cool. In a thick-bottomed pan, heat the ingredients for the filling to around 260 °F (125 °C). Dip the base of the pan in cold water to stop the heating process and divide the batter between the pastry shells. Garnish with fresh raspberries.

RASPBERRY SORBET

MAKES 8–10 PORTIONS

2 gelatin sheets
2 ¼ cups (500 ml) water
¾ cup (150 g) sugar
2.2 lb (1 kg) raspberries, defrosted or fresh
Fresh berries and sprigs of lemon balm, optional

Soak the gelatin in plenty of cold water. Bring the water
and sugar to a boil, then remove the pan from the heat.
Remove as much water as possible from the gelatin and stir
into the sugar mixture. Allow to cool. Using a spoon, pass
the raspberries through a sieve, pressing as much of the
raspberries through as possible. Mix into the sugar mixture
and freeze for about 40 minutes in an ice cream maker.
Garnish with fresh berries and lemon balm, optional.

CINNAMON WAFFLES WITH ORANGE BUTTERCREAM

MAKES AROUND 6 WAFFLES

BATTER:
1 ½ cups (200 g) flour
1 tbsp ground cinnamon
1 tbsp granulated sugar
1 tbsp vanilla sugar
2 eggs
6 ½ cups (400 g) lightly whipped cream

CREAM:
½ cup (100 g) butter at room
      temperature
2 tbsp confectioners' sugar
1 egg yolk
Zest of 2 oranges

Combine dry ingredients. Mix in the eggs and half of the lightly whipped cream. Carefully add the rest of the cream and let cool in the fridge for an hour. The batter is ready to bake using a waffle maker. To make the cream, beat butter and sugar until light and fluffy. Add the egg yolk and orange zest, and whisk for 3 minutes. Serve atop the waffles.

MILK CHOCOLATE SOUP WITH FRESH RASPBERRIES

SEE PHOTO, PAGES 34–35
MAKES 4 PORTIONS

½ cup (150 ml) cream
½ cup (150 ml) whole milk
3.5 oz (100 g) finely chopped milk chocolate
1 cup (100 g) fresh raspberries

Bring the cream and milk to a simmer in a pan. Remove from heat and add the chocolate. Mix using a hand-held blender. Divide into bowls and garnish with fresh raspberries. This soup can be eaten hot or cold.

TANGY LIME MOUSSE

MAKES 4 PORTIONS

1 gelatin sheet
2 egg whites
½ cup (100 g) sugar
The juice of 3 limes
3 ½ cups (200 g) lightly whipped cream
Lime zest to garnish

Soak gelatin in plenty of cold water. While stirring, warm the egg whites and sugar in a warm water bath, until it reaches a temperature of around 120 °F (50 °C). Using an electric whisk, mix until cool and add lime juice. Remove excess water from the gelatin, melt in a microwave oven, and mix melted gelatin with the meringue. Gently fold in the cream. Pipe into cylinders or serving glasses and let freeze for a few hours before serving. Garnish with lime zest.

CHOCOLATE MOUSSE WITH CARAMELIZED ALMONDS

MAKES 4 PORTIONS

1 egg yolk
1 egg
¼ cup (50 g) confectioners' sugar
3.5 oz (100 g) dark chocolate, melted
2 tbsp whisky
3 ¼ cups (200 g) lightly whipped cream

¼ cup (50 g) granulated sugar
1 tsp butter
Around ¾ cup (100 g) sweet almonds, blanched

Beat eggs and sugar until light and fluffy. Add the melted chocolate and mix thoroughly. Add the whisky. Carefully fold the lightly whipped cream into the mixture and mix till the mousse becomes smooth. Divide into serving glasses and refrigerate. To make the caramelized almonds, melt the sugar until golden brown. Add the butter and almonds and stir. Pour the mixture onto a baking tray covered in parchment paper and cool. Divide the almonds into chunks and use to garnish the mousse before serving.

MASCARPONE CREAM WITH SEA-BUCKTHORN

MAKES 4 PORTIONS

1 egg
¼ cup (50 g) confectioners' sugar
1 tsp vanilla sugar
4 cups (250 g) mascarpone
3 ¼ cups (200 g) lightly whipped cream
3 tbsp sea-buckthorn marmalade (check online, or substitute gooseberry jam or lemon curd)
2 tbsp water

Lemon balm to garnish

Beat the egg with the two types of sugar until foamy. Soften the mascarpone with a spoon and gradually add to the egg mixture. Fold in the lightly whipped cream. Divide between 4 serving bowls and cool for a few hours in the fridge. Mix the marmalade and water. Top each portion of mascarpone cream with a tablespoon of the marmalade mixture and garnish with sprigs of lemon balm. Serve chilled.

TIRAMISU WITH GINGERBREAD

MAKES 4 PORTIONS

12 gingerbread cookies, approx.
1 egg
¼ cup (50 g) confectioners' sugar
1 tsp vanilla sugar
1 ¾ cups (100 g) Philadelphia-style cream cheese
1 ¾ cups (100 g) crème fraîche
¼ cup (50 ml) Kahlúa

Cocoa to decorate

Crush the gingerbread cookies. In a mixing bowl, beat the egg and sugar until light and fluffy. In a separate bowl, combine the cream cheese, crème fraîche, and Kahlúa, and mix until batter is smooth. Gradually add in the egg mixture, stirring carefully. Layer the crushed cookies and the batter into glasses. Cool in the fridge for about 2 hours before serving. Decorate with cocoa.

SPICED, BOILED PEACHES

MAKES 1 ½ QUARTS

1.5-quart (1-liter) glass container with a lid that seals, such as a preserving jar (you may boil the jar before use to prolong the use-by date)

2.2 lb (1kg) peaches (around 6 peaches)
1 ½ cups (300 g) sugar
1 scraped vanilla pod
3 cinnamon sticks
4 star anises
4 small pieces of fresh ginger, approx. teaspoon size (5 g) each
2 ¾ cups (600 ml) water

Peel the peaches and cut into halves. Discard the pits. Bring all the ingredients for the sugar syrup to a boil, then lower the heat to a simmer. Add the peach halves and cover. Let simmer for 20 minutes. Remove from the heat and cool. Place the peaches and syrup in the glass jar and seal. Keep refrigerated. Serve with vanilla ice cream (see page 140) or lightly whipped cream.

CHOCOLATE TRUFFLE WITH ACACIA HONEY AND COOKIE CRUMBS

MAKES 4 PORTIONS

1 cup (250 g) whipping cream
5.3 oz (150 g) finely chopped dark chocolate
2 tbsp acacia honey

¼ cup (50 ml) melted butter
2 tbsp raw cane sugar
2 tbsp granulated sugar
½ cup (50 g) oats
½ cup (50 g) flour
½ tsp vanilla sugar

Bring the cream to a simmer and pour over the chocolate. Let sit for about 5 minutes. Add the honey and whip vigorously. Separate into serving bowls and let sit at room temperature for at least 5 hours. Combine the rest of the ingredients and mix until they resemble bread crumbs. Spread over a baking tray covered in parchment paper and bake at 350 °F (175 °C) for 15 minutes. Allow to cool. Sprinkle the crumbs over the truffle and serve at room temperature.

CANDY

NOUGAT ICE CREAM POPS

MAKES 6 PORTIONS

About 3.5 oz (100 g) nougat
Freshly made vanilla ice cream (see page 140)
3.5 oz (100 g) chocolate to garnish

Freeze some ice cream molds. Cut the nougat lengthwise
into 6 equal pieces. Cut each piece in half and sandwich
the popsicle sticks between the pieces of nougat. Place in
the freezer. Pour the freshly made vanilla ice cream into the
ice cream molds, until each mold is about halfway full. Press
the frozen nougat ice cream sticks into the container and
remove any excess ice cream with a spatula. Return the ice
cream molds to the freezer and let chill for about 3 hours.
Carefully melt the chocolate in the microwave oven on low
power, stirring occasionally. Remove the ice cream from the
molds by warming the molds with your hands. Place the
ice cream pops on parchment paper and pipe the melted
chocolate over them. Return to the freezer for a few minutes
before serving.

TANGY LEMON ICE LOLLIES

MAKES 6 LOLLIES

1 gelatin sheet
½ cup (100 g) granulated sugar
½ cup (100 ml) water
1 tbsp glucose syrup
Juice of 4 freshly squeezed lemons

Soak the gelatin in plenty of water. Boil the sugar and water, then remove from the heat. While stirring, add the gelatin and glucose. Allow to cool. Add the lemon juice and freeze the sorbet in an ice cream maker for around 40 minutes. Pour into pre-frozen ice cream molds—the molds should have been in the freezer for at least an hour. Return to the freezer and leave for at least 4 hours. Enjoy the finished ice lollies.

LIQUORICE TOFFEE

MAKES ABOUT 30 PIECES

1 cup (200 g) granulated sugar
¾ cup (200 g) whipping cream
¼ cup (100 ml) syrup
10 pieces of crushed strong licorice candy or 1 tbsp
   licorice granules
1.5 oz (50 g) chopped dark chocolate

1 baking tray measuring 5 x 5 inches (15 x 15 cm)
Oil for the baking tray

Edible decorative balls, optional

Heat the sugar, cream, and syrup in a thick-bottomed pan
until combined. Add the rest of the ingredients and heat to
about 250 °F (120 °C). Pour a drop of the toffee in a glass
of cold water to test. When the toffee forms a soft ball, it is
ready. Pour onto the oiled baking tray and cool. Cut into
½ x ½ inch (1x1 cm) pieces. Top with decorative balls and
store in a cool, dry place.

MARSHMALLOWS

MAKES ABOUT 30 MARSHMALLOWS

3 ½ gelatin sheets
¼ cup (50 ml) water
1 ¼ cups (250 g) sugar
3 tbsp glucose syrup
4 egg whites
3 drops lemon juice

Food coloring
Equal parts confectioners' sugar and potato flour to dust

Soak the gelatin in plenty of cold water. Melt the gelatin in a warm water bath or in a microwave oven until lukewarm. Boil the water and sugar with the glucose. Have a glass of cold water and brush handy so you can brush any sugar from the sides of the pan. Whisk the egg whites with the drops of lemon juice to form a light foam. When the sugar reaches 275 °F (135 °C), add to the egg whites while stirring continuously. Add the melted gelatin and whisk until the mixture cools. Add your preferred food color to the mixture. Pipe small cones of the mixture onto a baking tray dusted with confectioners' sugar and potato flour. Dust the top of the cones with confectioners' sugar and potato flour. Let stand for a few hours.

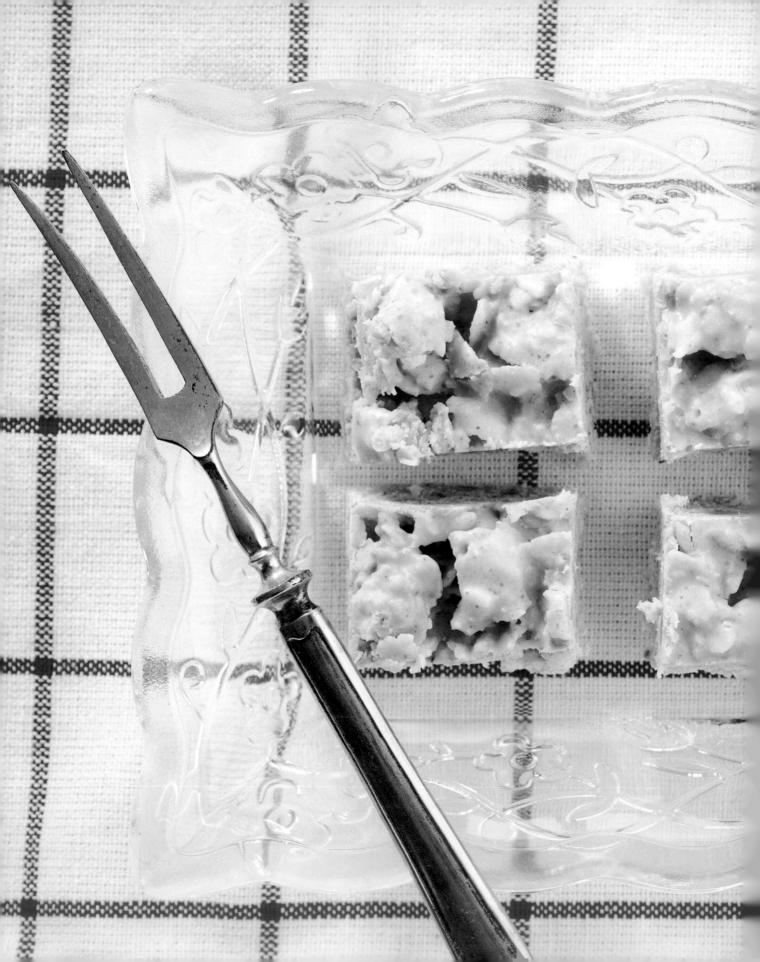

PEANUT CRISP WITH WHITE CHOCOLATE

SEE PHOTO, PAGES 58–59
MAKES ABOUT 30PORTIONS

3.5 oz (100 g) finely chopped white chocolate
½ cup (100 g) lightly toasted coconut flakes
3 ½ cups (400 g) corn flakes
3 tbsp peanut butter

Melt the white chocolate in a warm water bath or the microwave oven. Add the rest of the ingredients and stir. Spread the mixture into a rectangular shape onto parchment paper and refrigerate for a few hours to allow it to harden. Cut into small cubes and store in a cool, dry place.

PEPPERMINT-FLAVORED LOLLIPOPS

MAKES ABOUT 20 LOLLIPOPS

1 ½ cups (300 g) granulated sugar
1 tbsp glucose or white syrup
¼ cup (100 ml) water
½ tsp peppermint flavoring
2 drops red food coloring

Oil for the paper
Around 20 paper or wooden lollipop sticks

In a clean pan, heat sugar, glucose, and water to 260 °F (125 °C). This should take about 10 minutes. Remove from heat. Add the peppermint flavoring and red food coloring and stir. Quickly place the pan in a cold water bath (about 30 seconds) to cool the sugar. Spread the oil on some parchment paper and drop tablespoon-sized amounts of the mixture onto the oil. Immediately place a stick into each drop before the mixture hardens. Let cool.

PASTRIES

WHITE CHOCOLATE BROWNIES WITH PEANUTS

MAKES ABOUT 14 BROWNIES

½ cup (150 g) butter
½ cup (100 g) peanut butter
7 oz (200 g) finely chopped white chocolate
¾ cup (150 g) granulated sugar
1 tsp vanilla sugar
3 eggs
2 ½ cups (300 g) flour
¾ cup (100 g) salted, roasted peanuts

A 1.5-quart (1.5-liter) greased cake pan or 4 smaller cake pans

Melt the butter and the peanut butter together. Add the white chocolate and remove from the heat. Mix to form a smooth batter. Add the sugar and eggs—for best results, use a whisk. Fold in the flour and mix thoroughly. Line the bottom of a springform pan with parchment paper and secure the ring. Pour the batter into the pan and sprinkle with the peanuts. Bake in the center of the oven at 390 °F (200 °C) for 20 minutes. If using smaller pans, bake for about 15 minutes. Allow to cool. Serve with any of the sorbets or vanilla ice cream (on pp. 20, 23, 30, and 140).

VANILLA SPONGE CAKE WITH LEMON CURD

MAKES ABOUT 14 PORTIONS

¾ cup (175 g) unsalted butter
¼ cup (100 ml) milk
2 eggs
1 cup (200 g) granulated sugar
1 tbsp vanilla sugar
1 ½ tsp baking powder
2 ½ cups (300 g) flour
1 jar lemon curd, around ¾ cup (200 g)

A 1.5-quart (1.5-liter) greased baking pan or 4 smaller pans

Melt the butter in a pan on low heat. Add the milk and allow the mixture to cool. Using the highest setting of an electric whisk, whisk the eggs for about 8 minutes. Lower the speed to medium and whisk for 2 more minutes. Sift the dry ingredients through a fine sieve, and carefully fold them into the whisked eggs. Add the butter and milk mixture and stir. Pour the batter into the baking pan and bake in the center of the oven at 350 °F (175 °C) for about 40 minutes. Test the cake with a toothpick. When the toothpick comes out clean, the cake is done. Remove from the pan and allow to cool. Cut the cake lengthwise and smear with a thick layer of lemon curd. Replace the top half. (Another alternative is to bake in 4 smaller pans for around 25 minutes and pipe the lemon curd onto the smaller cakes.)

COFFEE-FLAVORED CHOCOLATE CAKE

MAKES 12 SLICES

2 eggs
½ cup (100 g) brown sugar
½ cup (100 g) granulated sugar
½ cup (150 g) salted butter, melted
7 oz (200 g) dark chocolate, melted
1 tbsp vanilla sugar
2 tbsp finely ground coffee beans
1 ¼ cups (150 g) flour
2 tbsp cocoa to garnish

A greased springform pan, around 10 inches (24 cm) in diameter

Combine the eggs, the two types of sugar, the butter, and the melted chocolate. Add the vanilla sugar and coffee. Using a fine sieve, sift the flour into the batter. Pour the batter into the springform pan and bake in the center of the oven at 350 °F (175 °C) for 30 minutes. Allow to cool. Remove the cake and dust cocoa over the top.

CHEWY ALMOND COOKIES WITH SAFFRON

MAKES ABOUT 50 COOKIES

1 ¼ cups (300 g) almond paste
2 egg whites
1 pinch (1/2 g) of ground saffron, dissolved in 1 tsp water
½ cup (100 g) granulated sugar to garnish

Soften the almond paste by working it with your fingers. Gradually stir in the egg whites. Add saffron and stir until well blended. Pipe the dough into small cones onto a baking tray covered in parchment paper. Top with sugar, shaking off any excess from the tray. Bake in the center of the oven at 390 °F (200 °C) for 8 minutes.

MADELEINES

⅓ cup (65 g) butter at room temperature
½ cup (100 g) sugar
2 eggs
1 ½ cups (200 g) flour
1 tsp vanilla sugar
Zest of half a lemon

A madeleine baking pan

Grease the pan carefully. Beat the sugar and flour to a light and fluffy batter, then whisk in eggs one at a time. Through a fine sieve, add the flour and vanilla sugar. Add the lemon zest. Pipe or spoon the batter into the baking pan, filling each well two-thirds full. Bake in the center of the oven at 350 °F (175 °C) for about 10 minutes if using small pans or 15 minutes for larger pans. Serve while still warm.

MILK CHOCOLATE AND COCONUT CAKE

MAKES ABOUT 14 PIECES

CAKE BASE:
4 cups (400 g) grated coconut
¼ cup (50 g) brown sugar
¼ cup (50 g) granulated sugar
3 tbsp light syrup
4 eggs

FILLING:
1 cup (250 g) whipping cream
1 tbsp glucose
9 oz (250 g) finely chopped milk chocolate
2 tbsp unsalted butter at room temperature

A greased baking pan, preferably square

Mix together all the ingredients for the base and spread the batter in
the pan. Bake in the center of the oven for 12 minutes at 350 °F (180 °C)
and allow to cool. In a pan, heat the cream and the glucose, and then
pour it over the finely chopped chocolate. Allow to stand for 5 minutes.
Add the butter and mix well. Pour the chocolate filling atop the cake
base and refrigerate overnight. Serve at room temperature.

CARDAMOM DREAMS

MAKES ABOUT 50 PIECES

¾ cup (200 g) unsalted butter at room temperature
1 ½ cups (300 g) granulated sugar
1 tsp vanilla sugar
1 tsp ground cardamom
3 cups (350 g) flour
1 tsp baking ammonia (available online and at specialty stores)

Beat the butter, sugars, and cardamom until light and fluffy. Add the flour
and baking ammonia and stir. Pipe small balls onto baking trays covered
in parchment paper (about 20 balls per tray) or into mini cupcake
papers. Bake in the center of the oven for 10 minutes at 300 °F (150 °C).

ALMOND AND CHOCOLATE BISCOTTI

MAKES ABOUT 30 BISCOTTI

½ cup (150 g) unsalted butter at room temperature
1 ¼ cups (225 g) granulated sugar
3 eggs
1 pinch of salt
3 tsp baking powder
5 ¼ cups (650 g) flour
7 oz (200 g) finely chopped dark chocolate

Mix the butter and sugar and add the eggs one at a time. Add the rest
of the ingredients and stir until a firm dough forms. Divide dough equally
into 3 parts. Roll each portion out to the length of a baking tray covered
in parchment paper and bake at 350 °F (175 °C) for about 15 minutes.
Cut at an angle into half-inch (1 cm) thick pieces. Return to the baking
tray, switch the oven off, and allow to dry in the oven overnight.

CUPCAKES WITH CHOCOLATE AND BEETROOT

MAKES ABOUT 24 CUPCAKES

1 cup (200 g) granulated sugar
½ cup (150 g) butter at room temperature
3 eggs
1 ½ cups (200 g) flour
½ cup (100 g) cocoa
1 tsp baking soda
1 ½ cups (200 g) finely grated beetroot (preferably fresh)

FROSTING:
¾ cup (200 g) Philadelphia-style cream cheese
3 tbsp confectioners' sugar
3 tbsp cocoa
1 tsp vanilla sugar
Edible decorations

Beat the sugar and butter until light and fluffy, and add in one egg at a time. Sift the dry ingredients into the mixture and stir. Add grated beetroot and mix together carefully. Divide the batter between the cake cups and bake in the center of the oven for 12 minutes at 375 °F (190 °C). Allow to cool. To make the frosting, use an electric whisk to whip the cream cheese, then sift in the rest of the ingredients. Whisk for another minute. Pipe or spoon the frosting onto the cookies. Garnish with edible decorations.

MERINGUES WITH RASPBERRIES

MAKES ABOUT 20 MERINGUES

3 large egg whites
1 cup (200 g) granulated sugar
¾ cup (100 g) frozen raspberries
A few drops of freshly squeezed lemon juice

Make sure the bowl and the whisk are clean. Whisk
the egg whites and lemon juice with a mixer on a low
speed for 3 minutes. Increase speed to the highest
setting and slowly add the sugar. Whisk until the
mixture forms stiff peaks and carefully fold in the
raspberries. Spoon the mixture onto a baking tray
covered in parchment paper, leaving a gap of about
2 inches (4 cm) between each one. Bake in the center
of the oven for about 1 hour at 230 °F (110 °C).

SYRUP COOKIES WITH ANISE

MAKES ABOUT 50 COOKIES

½ cup (125 g) butter at room temperature, salted
½ cup (100 g) sugar
1 tsbp vanilla sugar
1 tbsp white syrup or glucose
1 tsp baking powder
2 cups (250 g) flour
1 tbsp ground anise seeds

Mix together all the ingredients until a smooth dough forms, and divide the dough into 4 equal portions. Roll each portion out lengthways to fit onto a baking tray covered in parchment paper. Place each piece on the tray with a 2 ½-inch (5 cm) gap between them. Bake in the center of the oven for 8 minutes at 390 °F (200 °C). Immediately cut into 1-inch (2 cm) cookies.

HAZELNUT ALMOND CAKES WITH NUTELLA

MAKES AROUND 20 PORTIONS

½ cup (100 g) almond paste
¼ cup (50 g) butter at room temperature, unsalted
1 egg
1 tbsp flour
¾ cup (100 g) roughly chopped hazelnuts
1 jar Nutella
Edible decorations (optional)

Soften the almond paste by incorporating the butter, a little at a time. Add the egg yolk and mix thoroughly. Add the egg white and flour and mix until batter is smooth. Pour into baking cups or cupcake pans, until cup is 2/3 full, and sprinkle with hazelnuts. Bake in the center of the oven for 15 minutes at 350 °F (175 °C). Let cool. Top with a spoonful of Nutella and, if you wish, some edible decorations.

THIN TUILES

MAKES ABOUT 30 TUILES

¾ cup (75 g) unsalted butter at room temperature
1 cup (150 g) oats
½ cup (100 g) granulated sugar
1 pinch of baking powder
2 tbsp white syrup or glucose
2 tbsp cream

Mix together all the ingredients until well blended. Divide teaspoon-sized pieces of the batter onto a baking tray covered in parchment paper, leaving around a 3 ½-inch (7 cm) gap between each one. Bake in the center of the oven for 5 minutes at 390 °F (200 °C). Cool slightly, and fold over a small rolling pin to shape.

MILK CHOCOLATE BROWNIES

MAKES ABOUT 14 BROWNIES

¾ cup (200 g) butter

7 oz (200 g) finely chopped milk chocolate

1 cup (200 g) sugar

3 eggs

1 tbsp vanilla sugar

2 cups (250 g) flour

Confectioners' sugar and strawberries for garnish

Mix the chocolate into the melted butter. Add the sugar and eggs and stir thoroughly. Using a fine sieve, sift the rest of the ingredients into the bowl and mix. Grease a springform pan with a 10-inch (24 cm) diameter. Add the batter and bake in the center of the oven for 20 minutes at 390 °F (200 °C). Allow to cool. Garnish with confectioners' sugar and half a strawberry each (optional).

SOFT PINE NUT CAKE WITH HONEY

MAKES ABOUT 14 SLICES

1 ¼ cups (150 g) pine nuts
½ cup (150 g) butter at room temperature
¾ cup (150 g) granulated sugar
1 tbsp vanilla sugar
¼ cup (50 g) honey
3 eggs
2 ½ cups (300 g) flour

⅓ cup (50 g) pine nuts to garnish

A cake pan with a removable base, either a big one with an 8-inch (20 cm) diameter or two smaller ones.

Chop the nuts and whisk them together with the butter, the two types of sugar, and the honey. Add one egg at a time, stirring after each addition. Using a sieve, sift the flour into the batter and stir. Pour the batter into the cake pan and sprinkle with the nuts. Bake in the center of the oven for 30 minutes at 350 °F (175 °C). The cake can be served hot or cold. (Smaller cake pans reduce the baking time by 10 minutes.)

SIMPLE LEMON-FLAVORED CUPCAKES

MAKES ABOUT 12 CUPCAKES

¾ cup (200 g) almond paste
½ cup (100 g) butter at room temperature
5 tbsp flour
½ cup (150 g) Philadelphia-style cream cheese
1 tbsp confectioners' sugar
Finely grated zest of half a lemon

Pearl sugar or sprinkles to garnish (optional)

Combine almond paste and butter and stir until the mixture is smooth. Stir in the flour and lemon zest. Pour into small cupcake molds and bake in the center of the oven for 10 minutes at 350 °F (175 °C). Let cool. Whisk the cheese, sugar, and remaining lemon zest until fluffy, and then pipe onto each cake. Garnish with pearl sugar or sprinkles (optional).

QUEEN'S CRUMBLE

MAKES ABOUT 14 PORTIONS

¾ cup (200 g) butter, melted
½ cup (100 g) raw sugar
½ cup (100 g) granulated sugar
1 ½ cups (200 g) oats
1 ½ cups (200 g) flour
1 tsp vanilla sugar
¾ cup (100 g) raspberries, fresh or frozen
¾ cup (100 g) blueberries, fresh or frozen
¾ cup (100 g) strawberries, fresh or frozen

Mix together the first 6 ingredients until the dough resembles
fine breadcrumbs. Cover the bottom of an ovenproof dish with
about half of the crumble dough and top with the berries. Cover
the berries with the rest of the crumble dough. Bake in the
center of the oven for 50 minutes at 300 °F (150 °C). Crumble
can be served hot or cold with vanilla ice cream or vanilla sauce
(pp. 140 and 131).

COFFEE CHEESECAKE

MAKES ABOUT 14 SLICES

½ cup (150 g) butter
1 packet digestive biscuits, crushed, around 2 ¾ cups (around 300 g)
3 tbsp instant coffee
2 tbsp hot water
2 ½ cups (600 g) Philadelphia-style cream cheese
½ cup (100 g) sour cream
3 eggs
½ cup (100 g) granulated sugar

Spun sugar, raspberry coulis, and fresh raspberries to decorate
    (optional)

Melt the butter and add the biscuit crumbs. Cover the base of a springform pan, approximately 10 inches (24 cm) in diameter, with parchment paper and attach the ring. Spread the crumb mixture over the base. In a small bowl, combine the coffee and water and stir until dissolved. In a larger bowl, combine the cream cheese and sour cream with the sugar to form a smooth batter, and stir in one egg at a time. Add the coffee mixture and stir. Pour the batter into the springform pan and bake in the center of the oven for 50 minutes at 300 °F (150 °C). It should not have completely set and should still be soft in the middle. Cool before serving. Decorate with spun sugar (p. 148), raspberry coulis (p. 122), and fresh raspberries (optional).

SOFT GINGERBREAD WITH ROASTED WALNUTS

MAKES ABOUT 16 PORTIONS

3 eggs
1 ½ cups (300 g) granulated sugar
2 ½ cups (300 g) flour
⅓ cup (50 g) lingonberries
½ cup (100 ml) pouring cream, around 10%
1 tsp ground cloves
1 tsp ground cinnamon
1 tsp ground ginger
1 tsp vanilla sugar
1 tsp baking soda
¾ cup (100 g) roughly chopped walnuts

A 1.5-quart (1.5-liter) cake pan, greased

Mix together all the ingredients (except walnuts) until batter is smooth. Pour into the pan and sprinkle with nuts. Bake in the center of the oven for about 45 minutes at 350 °F (175 °C).

DELICATE CHOCOLATE SANDWICHES

MAKES ABOUT 15 SANDWICHES

DOUGH:
¾ cup (200 g) salted butter at room temperature
3 ¼ cups (400 g) flour
½ cup (100 g) confectioners' sugar
¼ cup (50 g) granulated sugar
1 egg yolk

FILLING:
½ cup (150 ml) whipping cream
3.5 oz (100 g) finely chopped dark chocolate
1 tbsp glucose or honey

Mix together all the ingredients for the dough until smooth. Cover in cling wrap and allow to rest in the fridge for at least an hour. On a floured surface, roll the dough out to roughly a quarter-inch (3 mm) thickness and cut out round cookie shapes, approximately 2 inches (4 cm) in diameter. Bake in the center of the oven for about 7 minutes at 390 °F (200 °C). Let cool. Heat the cream and, in a separate bowl, pour over the chopped chocolate. Add the glucose and mix with a handheld mixer. Let stand at room temperature for a few hours. Pipe or spread a little chocolate truffle on one side of the cake. Top with a second cake to form a sandwich.

PECAN PIE

MAKES ABOUT 16 SLICES

PIE CRUST DOUGH:
¾ cup (200 g) salted butter at room temperature
3 ¼ cups (400 g) flour
½ cup (100 g) confectioners' sugar
¼ cup (50 g) granulated sugar
1 egg yolk

FILLING:
¾ cup (100 g) finely chopped pecans
¾ cup (175 g) butter at room temperature
¼ cup (50 g) brown sugar
3 tbsp granulated sugar
1 tsp vanilla sugar
1 egg
¾ cup (100 g) flour

About 40 pecan halves for decoration

Mix together all the ingredients for the crust until
they form a smooth dough. Cover in cling wrap and
let cool in the fridge for at least an hour. On a floured
surface, roll out the dough to a quarter-inch (3 mm)
thickness. Line a tart form, that is about 12 inches (30
cm) in diameter, or two smaller ones, with the dough.
Whisk together the chopped nuts, the butter, and
the two types of sugar. Whisk in the egg, and using a
sieve, sift the flour into the filling, mixing thoroughly.
Pour into the lined forms and top with nuts. Bake
in the center of the oven for 25 minutes at 390 °F
(200 °C) for the larger pan, or for 20 minutes if using
smaller pans. Can be served hot or cold.

CHERRY CAKE

MAKES ABOUT 14 SLICES

¾ cup (200 g) butter
7 oz (200 g) finely chopped chocolate
½ cup (100 g) granulated sugar
½ cup (100 g) muscovado sugar
3 eggs
1 tsp vanilla sugar
2 ½ cups (300 g) flour

1 ¼ cups (200 g) fresh or frozen cherries, pitted

Whipped cream to serve

Melt the butter and remove the pan from the heat. Add the chocolate and stir. Add the two types of sugar and stir in the eggs one at a time with a handheld whisk. Using a sieve, sift the dry ingredients into the bowl and mix until batter is smooth. Grease a 1.5-quart (1.5-liter) cake pan with butter. Pour half the batter into the pan and cover with cherries. Top with the rest of the batter, and bake in the center of the oven for 25 minutes at 390 °F (200 °C). Serve with lightly whipped cream.

CINNAMON AND APPLE CAKE

SEE PHOTO, PAGES 108—109
MAKES ABOUT 14 SLICES

¾ cup (200 g) butter at room temperature
½ cup (100 g) granulated sugar
½ cup (100 g) brown sugar
1 tbsp vanilla sugar
2 eggs
1 tsp baking soda
2 ½ cups (300 g) flour
2 large cooking apples (for example, Jonagold)
1 tsp finely ground cinnamon
2 tbsp granulated sugar

Beat butter and sugars until light and fluffy. Add the eggs one at a time and whisk for another minute. Using a sieve, sift the baking soda and flour into the batter and stir. Line a springform pan, around 10 inches (24 cm) in diameter, with parchment paper and attach the ring. Pour the batter into the pan. Rinse and core the apples and cut into thin slices. Mix the apples with the cinnamon and the 2 tbsp of granulated sugar. Spread the apples on top of the batter and bake in the center of the oven for 1 hour at 300 °F (150 °C). Serve with one of the sauces or accompaniments that can be found at the back of this book.

ALMOND AND FIG TART

MAKES ABOUT 12 SLICES

¾ cup (200 g) almond paste
½ cup (100 g) butter at room temperature
1 egg
½ cup (50 g) flour
4 figs

Soften the almond paste and slowly stir in butter. Once batter is smooth and firm, add the egg and mix thoroughly. Add the flour and stir. Spread the batter over a greased tart pan with a loose base. Divide each fig into 4 pieces and place on top of batter. Remember to leave even spaces between each piece. Bake in the center of the oven for about 20 minutes at 350 °F (175 °C). Can be served.

WHITE CHOCOLATE CAKE WITH BLUEBERRIES

MAKES ABOUT 14 SLICES

¾ cup (200 g) butter
7 oz (200 g) finely chopped white chocolate
½ cup (100 g) granulated sugar
3 eggs
1 tbsp vanilla sugar
3 ¼ cups (400 g) flour
2 cups (300 g) blueberries, frozen

Confectioners' sugar to garnish

In a saucepan, melt the butter and chocolate. Add in the granulated sugar and eggs and stir thoroughly. Using a fine sieve, stir in the vanilla sugar and flour and mix thoroughly. Carefully fold in the frozen blueberries. Grease a springform pan, 10 inches (24 cm) in diameter, or a square pan. Pour in the batter and bake at the center of the oven for about 25 minutes at 390 °F (200 °C). Let cool.

BANANA MUFFINS

MAKES ABOUT 12 LARGE MUFFINS

½ cup (125 g) butter at room temperature
1 cup (200 g) sugar
2 eggs
2 ¾ cups (350 g) flour
1 tbsp vanilla sugar
1 tsp baking soda
½ cup (150 ml) milk
1 banana, mashed

Beat the butter and sugar until light and fluffy. Whisk in the eggs one at a time. Using a sieve, sift the rest of the ingredients into the batter and mix until well blended. Gently stir in the milk and the mashed banana. Fill each muffin cup three-quarters full. Bake at the center of the oven for around 20 minutes at 375 °F (190 °C). Let cool.

DAIM SQUARES

MAKES ABOUT 10 SQUARES

¾ cup (200 g) butter
7 oz (200 g) finely chopped milk chocolate
1 cup (200 g) granulated sugar
3 eggs
1 tsp vanilla sugar
2 ½ cups (300 g) flour
1 double Daim bar (can be purchased at Ikea stores), or
    alternatively 3.5 oz (100 g) Skor bar, chopped roughly

Cocktail toothpicks for serving

Melt the butter and remove the pan from the heat. Add chocolate and stir. Using a hand whisk, add the sugar and then the eggs, one at a time. Sift in the dry ingredients and stir until batter is smooth. Add the chopped Daim or Skor bar. Spread the batter onto a large baking tray covered in parchment paper. Bake in the center of the oven for around 10 minutes at 390 °F (200 °C) and let cool. Cut into 1 x 1 inch (2x2 cm) cubes and place a cocktail toothpick in each one. This is a perfect dessert to serve at a buffet!

WHOOPIE PIES

MAKES ABOUT 20 PIES

2 ½ cups (300 g) flour
1 tsp vanilla sugar
¾ tsp baking soda
1 ½ tbsp potato flour
½ cup (100 ml) cream
¼ cup (75 g) butter at room temperature
½ cup (75 g) granulated sugar
1 small egg
Zest of 1 lemon

CREAM:
¼ cup (75 g) butter at room temperature
1 tbsp confectioners' sugar
1 cup (200 g) marshmallow fluff
2 tbsp lemon curd

Confectioners' sugar to garnish (optional)

In a large mixing bowl, combine the dry ingredients. In a separate
bowl, mix the cream with the lemon zest. In a small bowl, beat the
butter and sugar until light and fluffy and add the egg, continuing to
whisk for a few minutes. Combine all the ingredients and stir until
batter is smooth. On a baking tray covered in parchment paper, pipe
the batter into 1 ½-inch (3 cm) pieces, leaving 2 inches (4 cm) between
each one. Bake in the center of the oven for about 7 minutes at 350 °F
(175 °C). Allow to cool. To make the cream, beat the butter and sugar
until light and fluffy. Add the marshmallow fluff and lemon curd and
mix until batter is smooth. Pipe or spread a layer of cream between
two cookies and garnish with confectioners' sugar.

ACCOMPANI-
MENTS

RASPBERRY COULIS

MAKES ABOUT 1 CUP (200 ML)

1 ¾ cups (250 g) raspberries, fresh or frozen (defrosted)
2 tbsp confectioners' sugar

Using a handheld mixer, mix raspberries and sugar. Pass
the raspberries through a sieve. Refrigerate. Raspberry
coulis pairs well with both cookies and ice cream. When
kept refrigerated, it will last for about 3 days.

FUDGE SAUCE

MAKES ABOUT ²/₃ CUP (150 ML)

½ cup (100 g) granulated sugar
2 drops freshly squeezed lemon juice
1 tsp butter
½ cup (150 g) whipping cream
1.5 oz (50 g) milk chocolate

Melt the sugar and the lemon juice until golden brown. Add the butter, then gradually stir in the cream. Pour the mixture over the milk chocolate and allow to stand for a few minutes. Stir and let cool.

BLACKBERRY COULIS

MAKES ABOUT 1 CUP (200 ML)

1 ¾ cups (250 g) blackberries, fresh or frozen (defrosted)
2 tbsp confectioners' sugar

Using a handheld mixer, mix the blackberries and sugar. Pass the blackberries through a sieve. Refrigerate. Blackberry coulis pairs well with both cookies and ice cream. When kept refrigerated, it will last for about 3 days.

STRAWBERRY COULIS

MAKES ABOUT 1 CUP (200 ML)

1 ¾ cups (250 g) strawberries, fresh or frozen (defrosted)
2 tbsp confectioners' sugar

Using a handheld mixer, mix the strawberries and sugar.
Pass the strawberries through a sieve. Refrigerate.
Strawberry coulis pairs well with both cookies and ice
cream. When kept refrigerated, it will last for about 3 days.

VANILLA SAUCE

MAKES ABOUT 1 ½ CUPS (300 ML)

½ cup (100 ml) milk
½ cup (100 ml) whipping cream
¼ cup (50 g) granulated sugar
1 vanilla bean scraped of seeds
2 egg yolks

Bring the milk, cream, 2 tablespoons of the sugar, and the scraped vanilla bean to a simmer. Remove the pan from the heat. In a separate bowl, stir the rest of the sugar (2 tbsp) with the egg yolks. Combine with milk mixture. Return the pan to a low heat and stir until the sauce thickens. Do not allow it to boil! Pass through a sieve and let cool.

WHITE CHOCOLATE SAUCE

MAKES ABOUT 1 ½ CUPS (300 ML)

3.5 oz (100 g) finely chopped white chocolate
½ cup (100 ml) milk
½ cup (100 ml) whipping cream

Place the chocolate in a bowl. Bring the milk and the cream to a simmer and pour over the chocolate. Let sit for about 5 minutes, then mix it into a smooth sauce. Can be served hot or cold.

DARK CHOCOLATE SAUCE

MAKES ABOUT 2 CUPS (500 ML)

1 ¼ cups (300 ml) water
1 cup (200 ml) granulated sugar
1 tbsp glucose or light corn syrup
¾ cup (150 g) cocoa powder

Heat the water, sugar, and glucose (or corn syrup). Add the cocoa and whisk thoroughly. Bring the mixture to a simmer. Pass through a fine sieve. Can be served hot or cold.

MILK CHOCOLATE SAUCE

MAKES ABOUT 1 ½ CUPS (300 ML)

3.5 oz (100 g) finely chopped milk chocolate
½ cup (100 ml) milk
½ cup (100 ml) whipping cream

Place the chocolate in a bowl. Bring the milk and cream to a simmer and pour over chocolate. Let sit for 5 minutes before mixing until sauce is smooth. Can be served hot or cold.

MANGO AND PASSION FRUIT COULIS

MAKES ABOUT 1 ½ CUPS (300 ML)

1 mango
¼ cup (50 g) confectioners' sugar
¼ cup (50 ml) cold water
2 passion fruits

Peel and pit the mango. Cut the flesh into small pieces and mix
with the sugar and water. Divide the passion fruit and remove the
flesh, including the juice and pips, and add to the mango sauce.
Serve well chilled. Mango and passion fruit coulis pairs well with
ice cream, sorbets, and chocolate cakes.

VANILLA ICE CREAM

MAKES ABOUT 1 QUART (1 LITER)

1 gelatin leaf
2 ¾ cups (600 ml) half-and-half
¾ cup (150 g) granulated sugar
1 vanilla bean scraped of seeds
5 egg yolks

Soak the gelatin in plenty of cold water. Heat the half-and-half with half the sugar and the scraped vanilla bean. Meanwhile, using a handheld whisk, mix the egg yolks with the rest of the sugar. When the half-and-half is lukewarm, take about ½ cup (100 ml) of the half-and-half and add to the egg mixture, stirring thoroughly. Return the egg and cream mixture to the pan and continue to stir. Remove from the heat. Remove excess water from the gelatin and add to the mixture while stirring. Chill the ice cream mixture in a cold water bath. For the best results, allow the mixture to rest in the fridge overnight. Pass the mixture through a fine sieve and freeze in an ice cream machine for around 40 minutes.

CHOCOLATE NETS

SEE PHOTO, PAGES 142–143
(STRACCIATELLA MERINGUE CAKE RECIPE ON P. 15)

¼ cup (100 g) finely chopped dark chocolate

Place a baking tray in the freezer for 4 hours. Melt the dark chocolate in the microwave. Prepare a cold plate, a spatula, and a piping bag with a small hole at the end. Fill the piping bag with the melted chocolate and, using the baking tray, immediately start to pipe the chocolate into a dense pattern. After about a minute, when the chocolate has hardened, lift it up with the spatula and form into a ball. Place on the plate and immediately refrigerate. Freeze the baking tray again for a few minutes and repeat the procedure to make more chocolate nets. Refrigerate for at least an hour before serving. Chocolate nets are easy to make and are a very impressive garnish suitable for all occasions.

LICORICE-FLAVORED TOFFEE SAUCE

MAKES ABOUT 1 CUP (200 ML)

½ cup (100 g) granulated sugar
2 drops freshly squeezed lemon juice
1 tsp butter
½ cup (150 ml) whipping cream
1 tsp licorice granules or 4 strong licorice candies, crushed

Boil the sugar with the lemon juice until golden brown. Add the butter
and the cream—a little at a time. Finally, add the licorice and heat for
another minute. Stir and allow to cool.

SPUN SUGAR

1 ½ cups (300 g) granulated sugar
½ cup (100 ml) water
2 tbsp glucose
A few drops of freshly squeezed lemon juice

Bring all the ingredients to a boil in a thick-bottomed pan. Make
sure you keep the edges of the pan clean by using a brush to paint
the sides of the pan with cold water. Boil until the mixture reaches
270 °F (132 °C). Place in a cold water bath for a minute. Cut the
wires on a whisk around the middle, so that the wires are about
half their normal size. Dip the whisk in the sugar and carefully
shake over some parchment paper. Repeat until you have the
desired amount. It takes some time, but it is well worth the
effort to make this pretty garnish. Spun sugar works
well as decoration on ice cream and cakes.
To remove the sugar when finished, soak
the pan.

COOKIE DOUGH

1 cup (215 g) butter at room temperature
½ cup (100 g) granulated sugar
½ cup (100 g) brown sugar
1 tsp vanilla sugar
1 egg
2 cups (250 g) flour, approx.
½ tsp salt
½ oz (50 g) finely chopped dark chocolate
½ (50 g) cup finely chopped pecan nuts

Beat the butter and sugar until smooth. Add the
remainder of the ingredients and stir. This cookie
dough works well as a mix-in for vanilla and
chocolate ice cream. It is also delicious to eat
as is. If you wish to bake into cookies, add 1 tsp
baking soda to the dough.

HAZELNUT SPRINKLES

1 ½ CUPS (200 G) BLANCHED HAZELNUTS

Chop nuts finely and roast in the oven at 300 °F (150 °C) for about 20 minutes. Stir every 5 minutes or so to allow the nuts to roast evenly. The nuts will taste so much better than anything store-bought, as these will be freshly roasted prior to serving.

MACADAMIA NUT SPRINKLES

1 ½ CUPS (200 G) MACADAMIA NUTS

Chop nuts finely and roast in the oven at 300 °F (150 °C) for about 20 minutes. Stir every 5 minutes or so to allow the nuts to roast evenly. Home-roasted nuts taste so much better than store-bought!

CHOCOLATE CURLS

APPROX 3.5 OZ (100 G) CHOCOLATE BAR—WHITE, DARK, OR MILK CHOCOLATE

Using a small knife or a potato peeler, pull the blade against the edge of the chocolate. Make sure you have some parchment paper underneath to collect the curls. Keep going until you have enough to decorate or flavor with.

PEPPERMINT SPRINKLES

Peppermint-flavored hard candy

With a sharp knife, chop the peppermint-flavored candy into the desired size.
Store in a dry place. These sprinkles work well as a
topping for ice cream or as cake decorations.

INDEX